READY TO FLY

PRAISE and WORSHIP for STUDENT CHOIR

Created by **DENNIS** and **NAN ALLEN**

PRODUCTS AVAILABLE:

Choral Book 0-6330-9345-9

Listening CD 0-6330-9347-5

Listening Cassette 0-6330-9348-3

Accompaniment CD 0-6330-9352-1
  (Split track)

CD Promo Pak 0-6330-9346-7

Cassette Promo Pak 0-6330-9353-X

Studio Charts 0-6330-9349-1

GENEVOX

Contents

Love Goes On

Words and Music by
MICHAEL BOGGS
Arranged by Dennis Allen

60's rock (♩ = ca. 118)

1st time: CHOIR unison
2nd time: GIRLS unison

1. I'm gon - na sing, I'm gon - na shout, I'm gon - na
(2. I'm gon - na) give, I'm gon - na grow, I'm gon - na

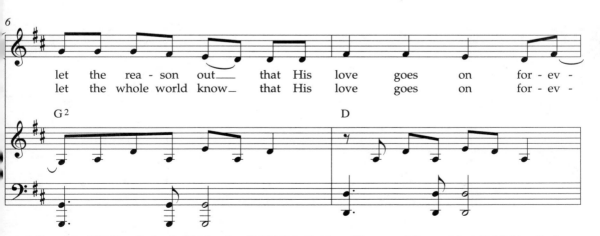

let the rea - son out___ that His love goes on for - ev -
let the whole world know___ that His love goes on for - ev -

GIRLS unis. *mf*

2. I'm gon-na ___ - ing me.___

His love,___ it has___ no end,___ it's long,___ it's wide___

___ and___ it's deep.___ His love___ has found___ a way___

into the ver - y heart of me.

I'm gon - na sing, I'm gon - na shout, I'm gon - na

let the rea - son out that His love goes on for - ev -

Ready to Fly

Words and Music by
J. DIEBLER
Arranged by Dennis Allen

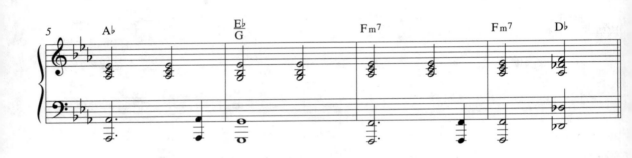

Traveling Light

Words and Music by
BROWN BANNISTER, MARC BYRD,
STEVE HINDALONG, and ALLISON MELLON
Arranged by Dennis Allen

Well, I was dou-bl-in' o - ver the load— on my shoul-der, Was a weight I car-ried with me

When I Survey

ISAAC WATTS

DENNIS ALLEN
Arranged by Dennis Allen

34

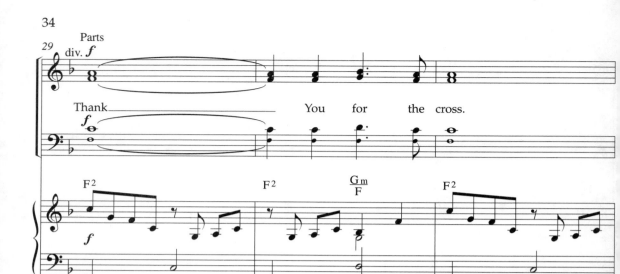

died.

When I sur-vey___ the won-drous cross, On which the Prince___ of glo - ry died.

Wonderful, Merciful Savior

Words and Music by
DAWN RODGERS
and ERIC WYSE
Arranged by Dennis Allen

42

You are the One that we praise,

You are the One we a - dore.

You give the heal - ing and grace   our

In Christ

Words and Music by
MICHAEL WEAVER
Arranged by Dennis Allen

Well, I may not be the great-est man to walk this earth,

but I know who is.

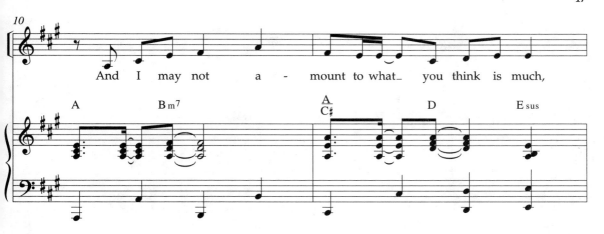

And I may not a - mount to what you think is much,

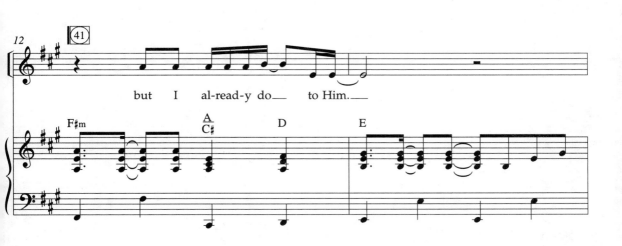

but I al-read-y do to Him.

While peo - ple keep search - ing for an - swers,

wants to live in-side__ of you.

In - stead_____ of search-ing an - y long - er

you can__ have peace_____ to - day,

Enough

Words and Music by
CHRIS TOMLIN and
LOUIE GIGLIO
Arranged by Dennis Allen

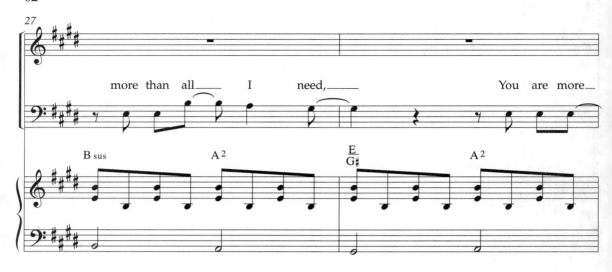

Who Is There Like You

Words and Music by
PAUL OAKLEY
Arranged by Dennis Allen

1st time: GIRLS unison
2nd time: CHOIR unison

Who is___ there like You?___

And who else___ would give their life for me,___

56 1st time
59 2nd time

E - ven suf-fer-ing in my___ place?___

1st time: CHOIR unison
2nd time: CHOIR parts

And who could__ re - pay You?__

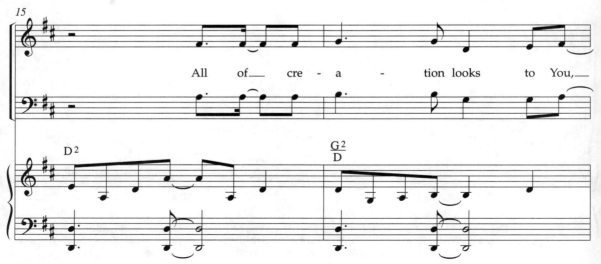

All of__ cre - a - tion looks to You,__

Word, trust-ing in Your cross, Trust-ing in Your blood and all Your faith-ful - ness. For Your pow'r at work in me is chang-ing me.

D2   Em7   D/F#   G   Em7   Asus   D2

Song of Love

Words and Music by
JEREMY ASH, MATT BRONLEEWE,
and REBECCA ST. JAMES
Arranged by Dennis Allen

moun - tains__ re-joice.__ The o - ceans__ cry,

"Al - le - lu - ia" As we wor - ship__ You, Lord,_____ As we

wor - ship__ You, Lord,_____ For this is our song__ of love.__

I Will Sing

FRANCIS H. ROWLEY

DENNIS ALLEN
Arranged by Dennis Allen

Rock

Words and Music by
DAVID JORDAN, KENT HOOPER,
and STEVE SILER
Arranged by Dennis Allen

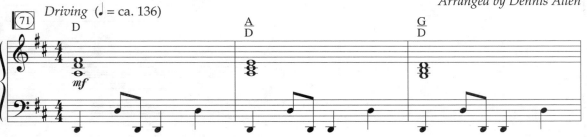

1. Lord, You are___ the sol -
2. I don't put___ my faith___

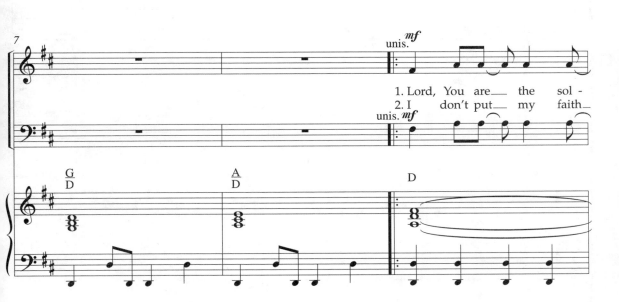

Welcome Home

Words and Music by
SHAUN GROVES
Arranged by Dennis Allen

Gath-ered on my search for mean - ing, And ev - 'ry clos - et's filled

— with clut - ter, Mess - es yet__ to be__ dis-cov - ered.

I'm o-ver-whelmed, I un - der-stand. I can't make this__ place all__

READY TO FLY

Sketches by Nan Allen

The following is a suggested order for a performance using songs and sketches in this collection.

Staging tip: Minimal set is needed. Hand props or a simple costume can create the proper environment.

Characters may start the sketch by turning their backs to the audience. They "enter" and "exit" by turning away from or toward the audience.

Choir: "Love Goes On"

Choir: "Ready to Fly"

TAKING FLIGHT

Scripture Reference: Hebrews 12:1-2

Characters:

AGENT: male; represents Jesus; an airline symbol pinned on a shirt or jacket could be a costume.

TRAVELER #1:   male or female; carries or rolls luggage, etc.; looks relieved to be surrendering baggage for the journey

TRAVELER #2:   male or female; carries or rolls luggage, etc.; protective of luggage and reluctant to surrender it

Optional Characters: Other TRAVELERS may stand behind TRAVELER #1 and TRAVELER #2; BAGGAGE ATTENDANTS may stand behind AGENT and take off bags to be checked.

Props: luggage, airline tickets, identification (2)

(Scene opens with TRAVELER #1 and TRAVELER #2 standing in line; AGENT enters at right and motions for next person in line.)

AGENT: May I serve the next person in line, please?

TRAVELER #1:   That's me.

AGENT: Welcome to Eternal Life Airlines.

TRAVELER #1:   Thank You. Here's my ticket and ID.

AGENT: Very good, Mr. Kinkade *(or real name)*. How much baggage will you be checking?

TRAVELER #1:   All of it. Everything I own I give to You. That's OK, isn't it?

AGENT: Sure. In fact, it's recommended. This journey is all about surrendering everything that might weigh you down.

TRAVELER #1:   What a relief!

AGENT: That's what we're here for. Flight boards at gate 7B.

TRAVELER #1:   Thank You. *(exits)*

AGENT: Enjoy your trip. Next in line. Welcome to Eternal Life Airlines.

TRAVELER #2:   Yes, here's my ticket.

AGENT: Good. Your ID, please.

TRAVELER #2:   Here.

AGENT: Mr. Winkler *(or real name)*…and you'll be checking all that baggage?

TRAVELER #2:   Uh, no. I hadn't planned to check any of it. I kind of want to hang on to it, if You don't mind.

AGENT: That's not possible.

TRAVELER #2:   Is it against regulations or something?

AGENT: Yes. You've gotta surrender it all. Just lay the baggage here. I'll take care of it.

TRAVELER #2:   I'm not sure I can do that. I mean, there's a lot of stuff in this baggage. And I've been carrying it for a long time.

AGENT: Oh? Like what?

TRAVELER #2:   Well, this one is filled with doubt, but I'm not sure...maybe I shouldn't have brought it. What do You think?

AGENT: Well, I think...

TRAVELER #2:   and this one is filled with fear...you know, the kind that's sort of paralyzing. I'm scared to let go of it.

AGENT: I see. What about that bag right there?

TRAVELER #2:   Oh, this? This one my mother gave me a long time ago.

AGENT: Oh, and what's that?

TRAVELER #2:   Guilt!!

AGENT: You've gotta give it up, you know, in order to take this journey.

TRAVELER #2:   Well, OK. *(gives three bags to AGENT)*

AGENT: And now that other bag.

TRAVELER #2:   Oh, this one is full of my *personal* belongings.

AGENT: Personal belongings?

TRAVELER #2:   Yeah, You know...*my* wants, *my* needs...*my* dreams.

AGENT: Sorry. Those have to be checked here, too.

TRAVELER #2:   What? Are You sure?

AGENT: Yes, but they'll be returned to you soon. I promise. Of course, they'll probably look different when you get them back.

TRAVELER #2:   Different?

AGENT: Yes, they'll actually be in better shape. It's about time to board. I need to know if you plan to go.

TRAVELER #2:   I don't know.

AGENT: You really need to surrender everything in order to take this journey.

TRAVELER #2:   What guarantee do I have that this will be a safe flight?

AGENT: *(hands Bible to TRAVELER #2)* Here's our customer service guarantee.

TRAVELER #2:   A Bible?

AGENT: I think you'll find that it is very interesting reading.

TRAVELER #2:   Yeah, I see. *(pauses to think)* You know, these bags *are* heavy—really quite a burden—I'm tired of trying to carry them myself.

AGENT: Let Me take them. I promise they'll be in good hands. *(AGENT reaches out, revealing His nail-scarred hands.)*

Choir: "Traveling Light"

Choir: "When I Survey"

RESCUED

Scripture References: Psalm 31:2; Galatians 1:3-5

Characters:

REPORTER #1:   male or female roving reporter; holds microphone and speaks to audience

RESCUED: female; stands at center surrounded by reporters, photographers, etc.; has a blanket draped around her shoulders

REPORTER #2:   male or female; holds microphone and interviews RESCUED

REPORTER #3:   male or female; holds microphone and interviews RESCUED

Optional Characters: Other REPORTERS may hold microphones or write on notepads as RESCUED tells story. PHOTOGRAPHERS may take pictures of RESCUED during interview.

Props: microphones (at least 3) All or some can be "prop" mics.; cameras (optional); notepads/pencils; All or some REPORTERS may write during interview.

(Scene opens with RESCUED sitting at center stage, perhaps on a stool; REPORTERS/PHOTO-GRAPHERS have gathered around.)

REPORTER #1:   *(enters and speaks to audience)* We interrupt this program to bring you live coverage of a daring rescue. We go now to a press conference for an account of the event.

REPORTER #2:   *(to RESCUED)* Miss Hindman *(or real name)*, tell us what happened.

RESCUED: Well, I was on this pleasure cruise.

REPORTER #3:   *(to RESCUED)* How long were you on the cruise?

RESCUED: How long? All my life really.

REPORTER #2:   That's a long time.

RESCUED: Yeah, it is.

REPORTER #3:   And you called for help?

RESCUED: Not at first.

REPORTER #2:   No?

RESCUED: No, at first I just drifted along, enjoying the ride—doing my own thing, as they say.

REPORTER #3:   Were you ever afraid?

RESCUED: A few times. But I was a Girl Scout, so I knew a few survival tricks, and…I took karate.

REPORTER #2:   So, you did fine for awhile?

RESCUED: Oh, yes, I was fine.

REPORTER #2:   Then what happened?

RESCUED: The sharks came.

REPORTER #3:   And that was when you called for help?

RESCUED: No, not yet. I still had a few tricks up my sleeve. Did you know that sharks really love thin mints?

(All reporters write feverishly.)

REPORTER #2:   No. That's good to know.

REPORTER #3:   So, then you drifted out further?

RESCUED: That's right—days…nights…days and nights. I lost count of how many. But my Father had me in His sights all along. He knew exactly where I was all the time.

REPORTER #3:   So your Father sent a rescue ship to get you?

RESCUED: No. It wasn't a ship.

REPORTER #2:   A helicopter?

RESCUED: No. Not a helicopter.

REPORTER #3:   Then how did your Father rescue you?

RESCUED: He built a bridge.

REPORTER #2:   A bridge?

RESCUED: Yep. Using Himself on a cross, He built a bridge to where I was and brought me home.

REPORTER #1:   *(to audience)* Amazing! You heard it here first, folks. Father sacrifices Himself to rescue drifting child. I'm Jonathan Treadway *(or real name)* for Channel 5 News.

Choir: "Wonderful, Merciful Savior"

Choir: "In Christ"

DAILY DELIVERY, PART 1

Scripture References: Matthew 6:11; Philippians 4:18

Characters:

COURIER: carries small box; may wear a hat with "Manna Delivery Service" on it

RECIPIENT: male or female

Props: small box

COURIER: *(pantomimes knocking on door)* Knock, knock.

RECIPIENT: *(pantomimes opening door)* Hello. May I help you?

COURIER: Yes, is this 4900 Franklin Road *(or real address)*?

RECIPIENT: It is.

COURIER: Are you Bryan Spillman *(or real name)*?

RECIPIENT: Yes, I am.

COURIER: I'm from Manna Delivery Service, and this is for you. *(hands over box)*

RECIPIENT: What is it? *(taking box)*

COURIER: It's from your Father—a lifetime supply of...uh, supplies!

RECIPIENT: Supplies? What kind of supplies?

COURIER: Everything you need...and then some!

RECIPIENT: But...

COURIER: Provisions for your body...your mind...your soul. Everything you really need to live...abundantly!

RECIPIENT: You said it was a lifetime supply. It's kind of a small box. This is supposed to last my whole life?

COURIER: No, this is just enough for today.

RECIPIENT:	What? Why?
COURIER:	It means you get what you need tomorrow…tomorrow. See you then. Have a nice day!

Choir: "Enough"

Choir: "Who Is There Like You"

DAILY DELIVERY, PART 2

Scripture References: Psalm 26:7; Psalm 95:2; Colossians 4:2

Characters:

COURIER:	carries small box; may wear a hat with "Manna Delivery Service" on it
RECIPIENT:	male or female
Props:	small box, letter/envelope

COURIER:	(pantomimes knocking on door) Knock, knock. Manna Delivery Service, making my daily run. (holds out box)
RECIPIENT:	(pantomimes opening door) Oh, great. Just in time. (taking box)
COURIER:	Here. Enjoy. (turns to exit)
RECIPIENT:	Thanks. Hey, wait!
COURIER:	Yes?
RECIPIENT:	Does it work both ways?
COURIER:	Excuse me?
RECIPIENT:	Both ways—you know, can you deliver something to my Father?
COURIER:	Sure. Anything you want.

RECIPIENT: *(takes out letter)* Here. Here's my thank-you note for all He's given me.

COURIER: Oh, OK. *(takes letter)* I'll be glad to deliver it…and I'm sure He'll be glad to get it.

Choir: "Song of Love"

Choir: "I Will Sing"

GREAT HOUSE

Scripture Reference: Matthew 7:24-27

Characters:

NARRATOR: male or female

BUILDER #1:   male or female

BUILDER #2:   male or female

STORMS: male or female (two or more); blow on houses like the big bad wolf

Props: blueprints or rolled up poster-sized paper; toolbox or toolbelt with hammer, nails, tape measure, small saw

NARRATOR: Once upon a time, there was a builder who decided to build a house. He gathered all the right tools.

BUILDER #1:   Blueprints, hammer, nails…

NARRATOR: The builder worked hard measuring…

BUILDER #1:   *(pantomimes measuring with a retractable tape measure)* 16…by 16

NARRATOR: sawing…

BUILDER #1:   *(makes sawing noises while pantomiming sawing wood)*

NARRATOR: hammering…

BUILDER #1:   *(makes hammering sounds while pantomiming hammering nails)*

NARRATOR: until finally…

BUILDER #1:   *(stands back and looks at house)* There! All done!

NARRATOR: It was a great house, all right.

BUILDER #1:   Great house!

NARRATOR: The nicest house on the block.

BUILDER #1:   Great house!

NARRATOR: However, even though the house looked great on the outside…

BUILDER #1:   Great house!

NARRATOR: It wasn't built to last.

BUILDER #1:   Huh?

NARRATOR: The house looked good, but it was built on an unsure foundation.

BUILDER #1:   A what?

NARRATOR: An unsure foundation. It was built on…sand.

BUILDER #1:   Oh, no!

NARRATOR: And so, over time, especially when storms came…

(STORMS enter.)

STORMS: We'll huff and we'll puff and we'll blow your house down! *(repeat two or three times)*

NARRATOR: the beautiful house began to fall apart.

BUILDER #1:   No!

NARRATOR: Until finally it was totally destroyed.

STORMS: *(make exploding and crashing sounds)*

(STORMS exit.)

BUILDER #1: (sadly) My…great house. (exits)

NARRATOR: But there was another builder…who decided to build a house.

(BUILDER #2 enters.)

BUILDER #2: Blueprints, nails, hammer…

NARRATOR: But before he began building, he made sure that he was building on a strong foundation.

BUILDER #2: (jumps up and down on stage) Solid. Hard as a rock.

NARRATOR: Oh, the house was lovely, too.

BUILDER #2: Great house!

NARRATOR: And no matter what happened…

(STORMS enter.)

STORMS: We'll huff and we'll puff and we'll blow your house down! (repeat two or three times; circle house and blow on it)

NARRATOR: no matter what storms hit, the house would not fall down.

STORMS: We'll huff and we'll puff and we'll…

STORM #1: oh, I feel light-headed.

STORM #2: Let me try…huff and puff…(blows)…huff and puff (blows)…I'm not even making a dent.

STORMS: (ad-lib frustration as they exit) Ah, man! It's too strong, etc.

BUILDER #2: Great house. Great house!

NARRATOR: Moral of the story: Be careful what you build your life upon. If it's built upon a foundation that could crumble, how will it stand up when the first problem occurs? But if you build your whole life on solid ground—on Jesus Christ—it's proven that—even when the storms come—it will stand forever.

Choir: "Rock"

A Sweet Deal

Scripture References: 2 Timothy 2:21; Ephesians 3:19

Characters:

BUYER: male; "Jesus" character

SELLER: male or female

Props: house key

BUYER: OK, Jimmy *(or real name)*, I'll take it. *(reaches for key)*

SELLER: *(almost gives key to Him, but pauses)* But, You haven't seen the rest of it.

BUYER: I know, but I'm ready to move in anyway.

SELLER: But...You might change Your mind when You see the other rooms, the places I keep hidden.

BUYER: I doubt it. When can I take possession?

SELLER: Uh...well, I'll have to make some improvements first.

BUYER: No, Jimmy, I'll take it like it is.

SELLER: But, You can't!

BUYER: I can make the changes Myself once I move in.

SELLER: Are You sure You don't want to think about it?

BUYER: I'm sure. I want to move in now. I'll pay an extremely high price, too.

SELLER: *(sighs)* OK. *(pause)* Here's the key. *(hands key to BUYER)* So, what do I do now?

BUYER: All you have to do is...move out! I'll do the rest.

Choir: "Welcome Home"

120